T0300707

George Sarantaris

Abyss and Song: Selected Poems

Translated from Greek
by Pria Louka

WORLD POETRY

First Edition, First Printing, 2023
ISBN 978-1-954218-09-3

World Poetry Books
New York, NY
www.worldpoetrybooks.com

Distributed in the US by SPD/Small Press Distribution
www.spdbooks.org

Distributed in the UK and Europe by Turnaround Publisher Services
www.turnaround-uk.com

Library of Congress Control Number: 2023931086

Cover design by Andrew Bourne
Typesetting by Don't Look Now
Printed in Lithuania by BALTO print

World Poetry Books is committed to publishing exceptional translations
of poetry from a broad range of languages and traditions, bringing the
work of modern masters, emerging voices, and pioneering innovators
from around the world to English-language readers in affordable
trade editions. Founded in 2017, World Poetry Books is a 501(c)(3)
nonprofit and charitable organization based in New York City, and
affiliated with the Humanities Institute and the Translation Program at
the University of Connecticut (Storrs).

Table of Contents

Introduction

THE POETRY OF GEORGE SARANTARIS springs from the fusion of worlds. Born in Constantinople in 1908 to Greek parents, and raised in Italy, Sarantaris was exposed from an early age to multiple languages: Italian and French at school, and Greek at home. His youth in Fascist Italy corresponded with major changes within the state of Greece resulting from the Greco-Turkish War (1919–1922). These changes included the annexation of several new Greek territories, as well as the influx of Greeks from Asia Minor. In an attempt to reconcile clashing perceptions of Greek identity, a group of poets, writers, intellectuals, and artists—mainly Greeks from Asia Minor—came together in the early thirties with the aim of forging a modern, cohesive Hellenic aesthetic through their creative work. They called themselves the "Generation of '30." George Sarantaris was part of this movement.

Though Sarantaris studied law at the Universities of Bologna and Macerata in Italy, his true passions were literature and philosophy. His parents wished for him to remain in Italy and get started on his career upon receiving his degree. Instead, he chose to return to Greece, where he ended up spending the rest of his life. Living off a meager income from rented family property, he devoted himself fully to poetry and philosophy. His arrival in Greece in 1931 coincided with the rise of the Generation of '30. A member of the Athens University Club, he led open discussions on philosophy along with his peer, philosopher Kostas Despotopoulos (to whom the poem "Philosophy" is dedicated). He was always on the lookout for emerging poets and would bolster them with his illuminating reviews and staunch poetic companionship. Among his "mentees" was Odysseus Elytis, who later won the 1979 Nobel Prize in Literature. His poetic style fit the ideal of the Generation of '30; namely that of a modernist aesthetic that nevertheless drew from Greece's ancient tradition. Sarantaris, channeling influences on his poetic development in Italy such as those of the French Symbolists (e.g., Charles Baudelaire) and the Italian Hermetics (e.g., Giuseppe Ungaretti), derived inspiration from traditional Greek tropes and themes, such as "garden," "sea," "sun," "sleep," "woman," and "death." The consistency of these themes, even within this sampling of poems, dated 1932 to 1940, reveals a highly developed, distinct poetic world, which nevertheless merges with the broader Greek landscape. Though Sarantaris wrote predominantly in Italian and French before moving to Greece, he displays profound awareness of the Greek language through play with syntax, grammar, and etymology. His simple, compact use of words recalls both the enigma of an oracle and the wit of an ancient Greek epigram. All in all, the aesthetic he developed spoke to his individual identity, while answering the quest for a new Hellenic one.

Sarantaris left behind a voluminous body of work, consisting of over a thousand poems as well as philosophical essays, critiques, and translations. Despite his prolific output and his active involvement in the Greek literary scene, he is treated as a marginal member of the celebrated Generation of '30. This is perhaps due to the fact that little of his work was published during his short life: only four slender self-published collections of poetry, and a handful of poems in literary magazines. Whether his work found an audience or agreed with others' sensibilities did not matter to the poet; he wrote out of necessity. Even while stationed at the front lines of the 1940 Greco-Italian War, he would busily scribble verse onto scraps. From the moment he decided to move to Greece and write in a new poetic language, to the moment of his death at age thirty-two, he was committed to developing his unique poetic idiom.

THE TITLE OF THIS SELECTION, *Abyss and Song*, taken from the first line of the poem "Anxiety," is a tribute to the dual nature of the philosopher-poet, who oscillated between the "abyss" of contemplation and the "song" of poetry. *Sing,* the poet ultimately exhorts (in a 1938 prose poem), *Do not cover up your voice with hands or words... let us recognize you by your voice alone, to love you...*

—Pria Louka, January 2023

Abyss and Song

* * *

Ἐγὼ δὲν ἀγαπῶ τίποτε ἄλλο
παρὰ οἱ μέρες νὰ γίνουν πιὸ μεγάλες
πιὸ ἀργές,
καὶ οἱ νύχτες πιὸ βαθειὲς
καὶ ἀπό τὸν ἑαυτόν μου νὰ μὲ κρύβουνε
σὰν ἄγγελοι σὰν θάνατοι γλυκοί.

* * *

I want nothing more
than for days to become longer
slower,
and nights deeper
so they can hide me from myself
like angels like sweet deaths.

* * *

Τώρα ποὺ εἶνε πλέρια ἡ γαλήνη
καὶ τὰ ἄστρα εἶνε κρίνοι
ἀπάνω στὴν ψυχή,
τώρα ποὺ λείπει καὶ ἡ σελήνη·
θἄθελα νὰ κλαίγω
τὰ ζηλευτά μου δάκρυα
μὲς στὰ δικά σου χέρια,
ὦ μακρυνή μου φίλη.

* * *

Now that calm reigns
and stars are lilies
upon the soul,
now that the moon too is missing,
I would like to shed
my prized tears
into your hands,
oh my distant friend.

Μνήμη καί σούρουπο

Σιγὰ περνᾶνε
ἀπὸ τὸν κῆπο ποὺ μᾶς ἐδέχτηκε
καὶ μᾶς ἔκρυψε ὅλη τὴ ζωή,
οἱ ὦρες οἱ γυναῖκες τὰ περιστέρια...

Memory and Dusk

Quietly they pass
by the garden that welcomed us
and sheltered us our whole life,
the hours the women the doves...

Ἀέρινη λεπτή, ἀνάλαφρη

Θυμᾶμαι. Θέλω καὶ θυμᾶμαι.

Ἡ ἀνάμνηση, μὲ τὴν ἀνατροφή,
ἀέρινη λεπτὴ γίνεται ἡδονή·
βασανισμένη, γοητεύει τὰ δάκρυά της
μὲ χαμογέλια· εἶναι
κι αἰσθάνεται τὸν ἑαυτό της ἡδονὴ
ἀέρινη λεπτή, ἀνάλαφρη...

Aerial Delicate, Light

I remember. Because I want to remember.
The memory, with nurturing,
aerial delicate becomes pleasure,
tortured, she charms her own tears
with smiles, she is
and she feels herself pleasure
aerial delicate, light...

Ἀνησυχία

Ἡ ὕπαρξή μου, ἄβυσσος καὶ τραγοῦδι,
πλανιέται στὴν κοιλάδα τῶν φαινομένων
Ὁ χρόνος τὴ δέχεται μ' ἐνθουσιασμὸ
μέσα στὶς ἡσυχίες του
καὶ τῆς προσφέρει χίμαιρες
τ' ἀπρόοπτα θεάματα τῆς γῆς
κ' ἕνα ἀληθινὸ πανόραμα,
τὸν οὐρανὸ

Anxiety

My existence, abyss and song,
roams the valley of appearances
Time receives it with euphoria
within his silence
and offers chimeras
unforeseeable spectacles of earth
and a real panorama,
the sky

* * *

Πεθαίνω· ἡ μέρα
τὸ ἐφύσηξε στ' αὐτιά σου·
πάρε τὴν ἀναπνοή μου
γιὰ καθρέφτη,
ὅπου μιὰ τελευταία
φορὰ θὰ μὲ
φιλήσεις.

* * *

I'm dying, the day
whispered it into your ear,
take my breath
for a mirror,
where one last
time you will
kiss me.

* * *

Άγαπάω τὸν ὕπνο
γιατὶ κι αὐτὸς ἀγαπάει τὴν ψυχή μου,
καὶ μοῦ σκεπάζει τὰ μάτια
μὲ τὰ λουλούδια ποὺ θέλω.

* * *

I love sleep
because it loves my soul in turn
and covers my eyes
with the flowers of my choice.

Φιλοσοφία

Στὸν Κώστα Δεσποτόπουλο

Συνομιλία μὲ τὸ ἀντικείμενο
πρᾶγμα μοναχό του·
σιωπὴ μετρημένη
ἀπὸ ἕνα ἄγνωστο αὐτὶ
μᾶς πλησιάζει
καὶ δένει,
γύρω μας βουίζει
μυθικὸ ἔντομο
ἕνας Θεὸς

Philosophy

For Kostas Despotopoulos

Conversation with the object
a lonesome thing;
deliberate silence
from an unknown listener
approaches us
and binds,
about us hums
a mythical insect
a God

Μῦθος

Ἡ σιωπὴ τῶν ματιῶν ἑνὸς ἀνέκφραστου κοριτσιοῦ
(*σφίγγα γεννημένη σὲ μιὰ χαραυγή*)
λικνίζει τὰ ἐρείπια τῆς αἰώνιας πολιτείας

Myth

Silence in the eyes of an expressionless girl
(born a sphinx at daybreak)
cradles the ruins of the eternal city

Άφέλειες

Μετέωρη μουσικὴ
διαλύεται ἡ ἐρωτικὴ στιγμὴ

λάμπει ἕνα δάκρυ σὰν ἀστραπή,
καὶ στὸν ἀφανισμὸ τὸ ἀκολουθεῖ
γλυκὸς τρυφερὸς πόθος
ἡ «συνεννόηση τῶν καρδιῶν»

32

Flyaways

For Miss P.R.

Music suspended
the erotic moment dissolves

a tear flashes like lightning,
and in vanishing is trailed by
sweet tender longing
the "communion of hearts"

* * *

Ὁ ἥλιος ἀκκουμπάει στὴν ἀπαλάμη ἑνὸς θεοῦ
ὅπου τὸ μυρωμένο φῶς του λυώνει·

μέσα στ' ἀνθρώπινα ὁ ἴδιος λείπει,
ἡ ἀνταύγεια τοῦ προσώπου του πεθαίνει

* * *

The sun rests on the palm of a god
where his fragrant light melts;

absent himself from human affairs,
the glint of his face dies

* * *

Σέβομαι τὰ δάκρυα
ποὺ ἀποσταμένα μάτια
στάζουνε σ' ἐπιφάνεια
ἀδιάφορη καὶ κρύα·
μάτια καὶ δάκρυα πᾶνε
ἔμβρυα τῆς ὕπαρξής μου
καὶ γίνονται διαμάντια
σὲ ἄλλον οὐρανὸ

* * *

I respect the tears
that drained eyes
drip onto a surface
indifferent and cold;
eyes and tears gone
embryos of my existence
and become diamonds
in another sky

* * *

Σπίτια χτίσαμε
χτίζουμε
καὶ εἶναι σκιὲς
ἀδελφὲς
τῶν ὀνείρων μας,
εὐαίσθητες
σὰν ψυχὲς

* * *

Houses that we built
that we build
are shadows
sisters
of our dreams,
fragile
like souls

***

Κάτι οὐδέτερο, ὅπως ὁ ὕπνος, ἀκολουθεῖ τὴν αἴσθηση
ποὺ ἔχω τοῦ κενοῦ καλύπτει τὸ φόβο της.

* * *

Something neutral, like slumber, follows after
the sensation I have of the void, hides the fear.

Σχέδια

Ἡ ἐντύπωση τοῦ φωτὸς δημιουργεῖ τὸν ὑπέροχον ἄντρα
ποὺ μοῖρα του ν' ἀρθρώσει τὴν ἀλήθεια
μὲ τὴν εἰλικρίνεια ποὺ φύλαξε ὁ νεκρὸς
στὸ μυστικό του

Designs

The impression of light creates the extraordinary man
whose fate is to articulate the truth
with the sincerity that the dead man kept
in his secret

* * *

Οὐρανὸς   διαβαίνει τὸν αἰθέρα
Ἡ πνοὴ ρέουνε τὰ χρόνια
Ποτάμια παιδιὰ μάτια
Ποὺ σταματήσανε εἰκόνες
Λόγια ποὺ περιγράψανε σιωπὲς
Ἀπὸ ζωντανὲς νύχτες

* * *

Sky   crosses the ether
Breath the passage of years
Rivers children eyes
That stopped images
Words that rendered silences
From lively nights

* * *

Τὸ σῶμα εἶναι ἔτοιμο
Ἄνοιξη ἄσπρο τριαντάφυλλο
Μιὰ σιωπὴ ἀπὸ σπουργίτια
Μάτια ποὺ πνίγονται
Διαγράφοντας τὴν ἀλήθεια
Λικνίζοντας τὸ μυστήριο

Λόγια μεστωμένα στὸ μέλι
Ποὺ κρέμονται ξέχειλα
Ἀπὸ οὐσία
Στὰ κλωνάρια τῶν δέντρων
Στὰ μπράτσα ποὺ σηκώνουνε καρποὺς
Τὰ χελιδόνια

* * *

The body is ready
Spring white rose
A silence of sparrows
Eyes that drown
Skimming the truth
Rocking the mystery

Words brimming with honey
Hang dripping
With essence
On tree branches
On arms that bear fruit
The swallows

* * *

Βλέπω
Ὥρα χαμηλὴ
Ἀνάστημα κόρης
Εἶμαι
Καὶ χάνω
Τὸ στόμα
Ξεχνάω
Τὴν ἁφὴ

Φάσμα
Ὁ χτύπος
Ἡ φλούδα
Τῆς ἀκοῆς

* * *

I watch
The small hours
Figure of a girl
I am
And I lose
The mouth
I forget
The touch

Specter
The thump
The husk
Of sound

* * *

Ὅταν φίλησα τὰ μαλλιά σου
Σὲ ἀγάπησα ἀληθινὰ
Σὲ γνώρισα
Σὲ ἀγκάλιασα μαζὺ μὲ τὸ κορμί μου
Σὲ πῆρα ἀπὸ τὸ δέντρο
Ἀπὸ τὴ ρίζα
Ὅπου γεννήθηκα κ' ἐγὼ

* * *

When I kissed your hair
I loved you truly
I came to know you
I hugged you and my body
I took you from the tree
From the root
Where I too was born

Ἡ ἔρημος

Οἱ πρωϊνὲς ὧρες μιᾶς ἐρήμου
Κόρη ποὺ κουβεντιάζει μ' ἔναν ἴσκιο
Ἴσως ὁ ἥλιος σέβεται τὴ σιωπὴ
Καὶ κάθεται σὰν τὸ νερὸ μιᾶς λίμνης

The Desert

Morning hours of a desert
Girl who talks with a shadow
Perhaps the sun respects the silence
And settles like the water of a lake

* * *

Μὲ τὴ διαύγεια τοῦ γιαλοῦ
Ξύπνα την τὴν κόρη!
Σ' ἕναν πόνο μυστικὸ
Ἔγειρε τὸ κεφάλι
Ἔκρυψε τὸ σῶμα
Σ' ἕνα σου φύσημα
Τ' ὄνειρό της λυγάει
Ξαλάφρωσέ την
Ἀπὸ τὴν ἡδονὴ
Κι ἀπὸ τὸν ὕπνο!

* * *

With the clarity of the seaside
Wake her—this girl!
Within a secret pain
She lolled her head
She hid her body
With a breath you take
Her dream buckles
Relieve her
Of this pleasure
And of this slumber!

* * *

Βαίνω πρὸς τὴ θάλασσα
Μὰ κυττάω τ' ἀστέρια
Βάρος στὸν καθρέφτη
Ὅπου ὁ πόθος μου
Μαρμαρυγὴ ἀπὸ τὰ ρίγη τοῦ νεροῦ

* * *

I head for the sea
But I watch the stars
Burden on the mirror
Where my desire
Glimmers from the tremors of water

Ἡ ὀμίχλη

Ἡ ὀμίχλη βρίθει
Ἀπὸ ἀνεμῶνες

Κοίτα τὰ κλαριὰ
Τί λίμνη
Τί ἀνυπόμονη καρδιὰ
Βλέπε μέσα
Στὴ σωστὴ σταγόνα
Ποιὰ φόρα
Παίρνει τὸ παιδὶ
Ποιὰ νάρκη
Ἡ γυναῖκα

The Mist

The mist teems
With anemones

Look at the branches
What a lake
What impatient heart
Peer into
The right drop
What drive
Takes the child
What languor
The woman

* * *

Ἐὰν δάκρυα μῦρα νιᾶτα
Ἀναπτύσσονται
Γέλα ἐσὺ φῦγε
Τὰ μάτια δίχως τρανὴ ἐλπίδα
Καὶ σ' ἕνα στόμα
Ὅλα τὰ λουλούδια
Ποὺ πίνουνε τὸ αἷμα

* * *

Should tears scents youth
Well up
Laugh get away
Eyes without grand hope
And in a mouth
All the flowers
Drink the blood

* * *

Κῆποι κῆποι
Πράσινη ὀχλοβοὴ
Μᾶς ἀφήνει
Ἡ νίκη
Ἡ πυκνὴ μυρουδιὰ
Θερμαίνει τὸν κόλπο
Σκεπάζει μιὰ χορδὴ

* * *

Gardens gardens
Green clamor
It leaves us
The victory
The thick scent
Heats up the womb
Muffles a cord

* * *

Αἰσθάνομαι ἀνάγκη νὰ τρώγω τὶς ἡμέρες
Ἔστω ἄγουρες

Ἡ ἄλλη τροφὴ δὲ λογαριάζεται
Παρὰ μονάχα ἀπὸ τὸ σῶμα

Ποὺ δυστυχῶς μοῦ εἶναι ξένο

Θέλω τὸ διάστημα τῶν ἡμερῶν
Ἐκεῖ τὰ χέρια μου νὰ πλύνω
Μέσα στὶς γυμνὲς ὧρες μιὰ ὑγρασία
Νὰ πῶ πὼς τρέχω κ' ἐγὼ μαζί τους
Ἐγὼ κι ὁ κόσμος

* * *

I feel a need to devour the days
Raw even

The other food does not matter
But for the body alone

Which is unfortunately a stranger to me

I want the stretch of days
To cleanse my hands there
Through the bare hours a moisture
To claim that I too flow with them
The world and I

* * *

Οἱ μέλισσες ἐγλύκαναν τὴν τύψη
Καὶ πήρανε τὸ ἔγκλημα στὴν πλάτη
Τὸ φέρανε στὴ λίμνη καὶ τὸ πνίξανε

Κ' εἴταν ζεστὴ ἡ ἀνάμνηση τοῦ ὕπνου

* * *

The bees sweetened remorse
And they took the crime on their back
They carried it to the lake and drowned it

And it was warm, the remembrance of sleep

* * *

Σκούπισε τὸν ὕπνο σελήνη
Ἀπὸ τὰ σώματα
Βάλε τὸν ὕπνο στὴν κρήνη

. . .

Κελαϊδιστὰ ἡ ὥρα
Θὰ μᾶς πλύνει
Ἀπὸ τὸ θόρυβο

* * *

Dust sleep, moon,
Off the bodies
Place sleep in the spring

. . .

Trilling, the hour
Will cleanse us
Of the noise

* * *

Ἡ αὐγὴ ἀγάπησε
Κάτι σὰν τὸ κορίτσι
Ποὺ δὲ γεννήθηκε ποτέ,

Καὶ μίλησε
Φίλησε
Τὰ μαλλιὰ τοῦ κοριτσιοῦ

Πιὸ λαμπρὰ ἀπὸ τὴ χλόη
Ἀπὸ τὸ μοσκοβόλημα
Τῆς γῆς

* * *

Dawn loved
Something like the girl
Who was never born,

And spoke
Kissed
The girl's hair

Brighter than fresh grass
Than the sweet scent
Of earth

* * *

Ἀλαφροέρχονται οἱ σκιὲς τοῦ ἄλλου κόσμου
Ὅταν οἱ δροσιὲς τοῦ κήπου
Γιὰ λίγην ὥρα
Δὲ μᾶς ραντίζουν

* * *

Shadows of the other world drift in
When the garden's mists
For a little while
Cease to sprinkle us

Οἱ μενεξέδες

Τὰ φῶτα σὰν πουκάμισα
Ντύνουν τὰ σώματα
Ἐκείνων τῶν ἀνθρώπων
Ποὺ ἀγαπήσαμε
Καὶ ποὺ ἀφήσαμε
Ἢ μᾶς ἀφῆκαν
Χωρὶς χαιρετισμὸ

Ποτὲ δὲν καρτερούσαμε
Τέτοιο θέαμα
Δὲν προέβλεπαν
Τὰ μάτια μας
Τόσους κρίνους

Εἶταν γραφτὸ νὰ χάσουμε τὸν ὕπνο
Χωρὶς διαμαρτυρία
Μέσα στοὺς μενεξέδες νὰ σκορπίσουμε
Καὶ νὰ ξαναβρεθοῦμε

74

The Violets

Lights like garments
Dress the bodies
Of those
Whom we loved
And whom we left
Or who left us
Without a goodbye

Never did we expect
Such a spectacle
Our eyes
Did not foresee
So many lilies

We were destined to lose sleep
Without protest
To scatter among violets
And meet again

* * *

Στὴ θάλασσά μας πέσανε βροχὲς
Λίγες βροχὲς καὶ λίγα περιστέρια

* * *

Rains fell upon our sea
Few rains and few doves

Ἄσπρες ἰδέες

Ἡ νύχτα δὲ μᾶς ἔκλεψε τὸ σῶμα
Ἡ νύχτα ἀνεμίζει ἄσπρες ἰδέες
Ὁ καιρὸς ἀπόψε δὲν εἶναι σπάνιος
Καὶ δὲν εἶναι ὀχληρὸς
Εἶναι ὁ ἀμύθητος ἀνατολίτικος κῆπος
Ποὺ τὴν εὐγνωμοσύνη μας ἐκέρδισε
Μέσα σὲ ὄνειρο
Καὶ τώρα παρουσιάζεται σὰν ἥρωας
Μιᾶς ἱστορίας ἀλλοτινῆς
Σὰν ἐξουσιαστὴς ἑνὸς κόσμου
Ποὺ ἀπομακραίνεται
Ὅμως κυκλοφοροῦμε μέσα του χωρὶς ἐνδοιασμοὺς
Τὰ λόγια μας σηκώνουν τ' ἀντικείμενα
Τὰ τοποθετοῦν σὲ ράφια
Ἔχουμε πλησιάσει πρὸς τὸ φῶς
Ἐνῶ δὲν προσέχαμε τὸ πράμα τῆς ζωῆς μας
Ἔχουμε γίνει ἥλιος μὲ τὸν ἥλιο
Καὶ δὲν εἴδαμε τὸ χρόνο νὰ περνᾶ
Ν' ἁπλώνει τὸ γῦρο του
Νὰ χορεύει μαζὶ μὲ τοὺς ἀνθρώπους
Νὰ χορεύει μὲ μᾶς τοὺς ἴδιους
Ποὺ σκεπτόμαστε μονάχα τὸ φῶς
Μονάχα τὸ φῶς βλέπαμε
Καὶ δὲν ξέραμε ἄλλο τίποτα
Μήτε τὰ βήματά μας μὲς στὴν ὕλη
Μήτε τὴν ἡδονή μας μὲ τὴν ὕλη
Μήτε τὸ χρόνο ἐκεῖνο ποὺ δὲν εἶναι σύννεφο
Δὲν εἶναι μουσικὴ μέσα στὸν ἥλιο
Δὲν εἶναι χαρὰ μέσα στὸ φῶς

White Ideas

Night did not possess our body
Night waves white ideas
Time is not rare tonight
Nor is it bothersome
It's the boundless oriental garden
That earned our gratitude
Within a dream
And now appears as the hero
Of an old tale
The ruler of a world
Growing distant
Where we nevertheless circulate without qualms
Our words pick up the objects
Place them on shelves
We have come toward the light
While neglecting the substance of our life
We have become sun with the sun
And did not notice time pass
Expanding its circle
Dancing with people
Dancing with us even
Who think only of the light
Only the light we saw
And we knew nothing else
Neither of our steps through matter
Nor of our pleasure with matter
Nor of that time which is not cloud
Not music in the sun
Not joy in the light

* * *

Κάμε χῶρο εἶμαι ἕνας
Πού σπρώχνει τόν ἄνεμο
Ἕνας πού στή ράχη του
Φέρνει βουνά
Γιά νά καθήσουν πουλιά
Καί κελαϊδήσουν

* * *

Make way I am one
Who shoves the wind
One who bears mountains
On his back
For birds to sit
And sing

* * *

Ἡ θάλασσα σηκώνει τὰ δάχτυλα καὶ περιαυτολογεῖ
Ὄρθιο τὸ βουνὸ χάνεται μέσα στὰ σύννεφα

* * *

The sea lifts her fingers and brags
Upright, the mountain fades behind clouds

* * *

Ἄφησες τὰ μαλλιά σου νὰ τρέχουν πάνω στὴ θάλασσα
Καὶ τὰ κύματα τὰ χαϊδεύουν

Ὁ ἥλιος ἔφυγε
Ἀλλὰ ἡ μέρα σταμάτησε τὴν πορεία της
Καὶ κυττάζει τὰ μαλλιά σου

Ἀγέρες κατεβαίνουν ἀπ' τὸ βουνὸ
Κάθονται στὸ γιαλὸ
Καὶ γύρους κάνουν τὶς φωνές τους
Γιὰ νὰ σὲ πιάσουν
Τώρα ποὺ ζυγώνεις τὴ στεριὰ
Καὶ τρέμεις σὰν τὸ σύννεφο

Ἄφησε τὴ λαλιά σου νὰ κελαϊδήσει
Πάλι θ' ἀστράψουν οἱ βράχοι
Πάνω τους θὰ μαζευτεῖ ἡ ζωή μας
Γιὰ νὰ σὲ κλείσει στὸ στῆθος

* * *

You let your hair loose over the sea
And the waves caress it

The sun has gone
But the day stopped in its tracks

And watches your hair

Winds descend from the mountain
They settle on the shore
And make their voices go round
To catch you
Now that you approach dry land
And you tremble like the cloud

Loosen your tongue and sing
The rocks will gleam again
Our life will gather upon them
To enclose you in embrace

* * *

Τοῦ κόπου καὶ τοῦ μόχθου τῶν περιστεριῶν
Στάθηκα ἐραστὴς

Γιατὶ μοῦ φάνηκε πὼς ἡ ζωὴ τ' οὐρανοῦ
Κύλησε ἴσαμε τὸ στῆθος τῶν πουλιῶν

Καὶ πιὰ δὲν εἶχα ὄρεξη νὰ μάθω
Ὀνόματα χωρῶν
Πρόσωπα
Πράματα

Δὲ μὲ τραβοῦσε τὸ κελάδημα τῆς γῆς
Ὅταν δὲν ἀνεβαίνει

Πάνω ἀπ' τὰ δέντρα
Ὁ ψίθυρος τῆς πλάσης γελαστὸς
Τὰ σώματά μας λάμπουνε περίφημα
Σὲ τέτοιες ὄασεις

Καὶ ἀκοντίζουν ὑπέροχες κραυγὲς
Τόσες ποὺ τὰ πουλιὰ δὲ λησμονᾶνε
Τὸ ἄρωμα τὸ μοσχοβόλημα τῆς χλόης

* * *

Of the efforts and the toil of the doves
I proved a lover

Because it seemed to me that the life of the sky
Rolled up to the breast of the birds

And I no longer sought to learn
Names of countries
Faces
Things

I was not lured by the earth's call
When not rising

Above the treetops
The beaming whisper of creation
Our bodies glow exalted
In such oases

And spear exuberant cries
So many that the birds do not forget
The fragrance the lusciousness of grass

* * *

Ὑπάρχει ἕνας καθρέφτης μέσα μας· εἶναι ὁ ἥλιος.

* * *

There is a mirror within us: the sun

* * *

Νοερὰ διαμάντια
Κελαϊδάει ὁ νοῦς μου

Μέσα στὴ νύχτα
Στολίστηκε ἡ παρθένα
Καὶ τὴν ἀκολουθοῦσε
Ὁ χτύπος τῆς καμπάνας
Τὴ χαιρετοῦσε
Ὁ νόμος τῆς καρδιᾶς μου
Παράμερα ἡ ἄνοιξη
Εἶχε ἀφρίσει

Μόνο θυμᾶμαι ἐσένα
Εἶχες φύγει
Εἶχες φύγει
Γλυκύτατη παρθένα
Ἡ φωνή σου ἀκούγονταν
Σὰν ἄστρο
Τὸ ἄρωμά σου πετοῦσε
Σὰ λειβάδι

* * *

Inner diamonds
My mind sings

In the night
The virgin adorned herself
And was followed
By the toll of the bell
She was greeted
By the rule of my heart
Off to the side spring
Frothed

I remember only you
You fled
You fled
Sweetest maiden
Your voice sounded
Like a star
Your perfume soared
Like a meadow

* * *

Κόβεις ἕνα δέντρο
Καὶ εἶναι σὰ νὰ κόβεις
Ἕνα δάχτυλο,
Γίνεται μέλι
Τὸ δέντρο,
Γίνεται κάποτε
Πουλί,
Ἀλλὰ τότε
Σὲ ἀποχαιρετᾶ

* * *

You chop down a tree
And it's as though you chop
A finger,
Becomes honey
The tree
At some point becomes
Bird,
But then
Bids you farewell

* * *

Ἔχω κάποτε λιγάκι ὄρεξη νὰ κοιμηθῶ μὲ τὰ
πουλιά, ἂν καὶ τὰ πουλιὰ δὲν τὰ εἶδα ποτέ μου· ποτέ μου
ἀπὸ κοντά· δὲν εἶδα κατὰ ποιὸν τρόπο κατεβά—
ζουν τὰ φτερά, κι ἀφήνουν τὸν οὐρανὸ καὶ τρέχει.

* * *

I sometimes wish to sleep with the birds,
though I have never seen the birds—never up
close—I have not seen how they lower their wings,
and let the sky flow.

* * *

Μπορεῖ νὰ πεῖ κανεὶς πὼς ὄχι ὅλος ὁ ἑαυτός μας κοιμᾶται· ἡ ποίηση εἶναι ἐκεῖνος ὁ ἑαυτός μας ποὺ δὲν κοιμᾶται ποτέ.

* * *

One could say that we are never fully asleep—
poetry is the self that never sleeps.

* * *

Ἔλα ἥλιε αὐτί μου
Ἔλα νὰ δοῦμε λιγάκι τὸ νοῦ

Φεγγοβολάει τὴ θάλασσα
Ἀπὸ τ' ἄστρα γυρίζει

Κάποια χώρα γεννάει
Κάποια χώρα λειβάδια
Ἀλώνια περβόλια
Καὶ ἡ δική μας σιωπὴ
Τὰ ξυπνάει
Στὴν ἀγκαλιὰ τῆς γῆς
Ἀνάμεσα σ' οὐρανοὺς καὶ νερὰ
Καὶ ὁμιλίες ποὺ λαμποκοποῦν
Μὲ τόσα φτερὰ

Μὲ τέτοιο σκίρτημα κανεὶς δὲ φεύγει
Κανεὶς δὲν κοιμᾶται
Μὲ τέτοιο δάσος καρδιῶν
Κανεὶς δὲν προχωρεῖ στὸν ἄνεμο
Μ' ἐλαφρότερο βῆμα
Κανεὶς ποτὲ δὲν πήδηξε
Τοῦ θανάτου τὴν ἄβυσσο

* * *

Come sun, my ear
Come take a peek at the mind

It illumines the sea
It orbits the stars

It gives birth to some country
Some country some meadows
Fields orchards
And our silence
Awakens them
In earth's embrace
Between skies and waters
And voices that flash
With so many wings

With such a quiver no one leaves
No one sleeps
With such a thicket of hearts
No one proceeds into the wind
With a lighter gait
No one ever leapt
Over the abyss of death

* * *

Δίχως τέλος οἱ γλάροι βλέπουν τὴ θάλασσα
Μονόχρωμη

Κ' ἡ ἄρπα μὲ τὴ μουσική της
Ἀγκαλιάζει τὸν ἀγέρα

Ὁ ἀφρὸς ἀνεβαίνει
Τὰ κόκκαλα τῶν ζώων γίνονται ἀρώματα

Ὦ θαλπωρὴ τοῦ ἀνθρώπου στὸ πέλαγος
Ἐξαίσιος θρύλος!

* * *

Endlessly the gulls watch the sea
Monochrome

The harp with her music
Hugs the wind

The foam ascends
The bones of beasts become fragrances

Oh human warmth on the open sea
Extraordinary legend!

* * *

Ὁ ἥλιος ποὺ μεσουρανεῖ

Ἐδῶ ἦρθα μὲ τὴν ἀγάπη μου

Κύττα ἐκεῖνο τὸ μαντῆλι
Ἐκεῖνο τὸ μαντεῖο τῶν Δελφῶν!

Βλέπω τὸ παιχνίδι
Καὶ δὲν παίζω πιὰ
Ἡ μουσικὴ παίζει γιὰ μένα
Ὅλων τῶν λουλουδιῶν ἡ μουσικὴ
Κι ὅλα τὰ στόματα τρῶνε τοὺς καρποὺς
Ὁ κῆπος ἄδειασε
Οἱ ἐραστὲς καὶ τ' ἀγάλματα
Φύγανε
Ἡ χλόη ἀνέβηκε
Ὅπως οἱ κολῶνες τοῦ καπνοῦ

Κύττα πῶς εἶναι ἀνάλαφρο τὸ δέρμα
Ἀνάμεσα ἀπ' τὰ σώματα διακρίνουμε
Πότε τὸν ἥλιο
Πότε τὸ φεγγάρι

* * *

The sun at its zenith

I came here with my love

See that veil
That oracle of Delphi!

I watch the game
And I no longer play
The music plays for me
The music of all flowers
And all the mouths gorge on fruit
The garden has emptied
The lovers and the statues
Left
The grass rose
Like columns of smoke

See how the skin is borne lightly
Among the bodies we discern
Sometimes the sun
Sometimes the moon

* * *

Ὁ θάνατος
Πιὸ ἐλαφρὸς κι ἀπὸ ἕνα φτερὸ
Ἔδειξε τὸν ἥλιο
Καὶ εἶπε στὸν ἑαυτό του
Πήγαινέ με ἀπάνω
Νὰ πεθάνω ἐκεῖ
Ἀνάμεσα στ' ἀρώματα τῶν λουλουδιῶν
Ποὺ φαίνεται δὲ σβύνουν
Καὶ μὲ τὸν πράσινο κισσὸ τῆς μοίρας
Παντοτεινὰ νὰ λούζομαι
Στὸ βλέμμα ἑνὸς ἀνθρώπου

* * *

Death
Lighter than even a feather
Pointed to the sun
And said to himself
Take me up there
To die
Amid the fragrances of flowers
That seem never to fade
And with the green ivy of fate
Forever to bathe
In a human gaze

* * *

Τούτη ἡ φωνὴ εἶναι βαθειὰ σὰ λουλούδι

Μὴν τὴν μολύνεις· θὰ σοῦ πεῖ τὸ πρόσωπό σου
Ὅταν ἀστράφτει πάνω ἀπ' τοὺς γύρους τοῦ καιροῦ

. . .

Μὴν πετάξεις προτοῦ ἡ δίψα σου γράψει τὸ οὐράνιο τόξο
Καὶ οἱ πετεινοὶ ἐπαινέσουν τ' ὄνομά σου

* * *

This voice is deep like a flower

Don't taint it—it will reveal your face
When it shines above the circuit of time

. . .

Don't fly off until your thirst scribes the rainbow
And the roosters laud your name

* * *

Νὰ τὰ φᾶμε ἢ νὰ τὰ πιοῦμε τ' ἄστρα;

* * *

Should we eat or should we drink the stars?

Bibliographical Note

Poems published by the poet in self-published collections include "Aerial Delicate, Light," in *Loves of time* (*Οἱ ἀγάπες τοῦ χρόνου*, 1933), and "Anxiety," "Philosophy," "Myth," and "Flyaways," in *Celestials* (*Τὰ οὐράνια*, 1934). The poems "The Mist" and [There is a mirror within us...] were first published in literary magazines *Nea Grammata* (vol. 3, no. 3, March 1937, p. 199–202) and *Nea Estia* (vol. 27, no. 216, Feb. 1940, p. 27), respectively.

The rest of the poems in this publication are based on the poet's handwritten manuscripts preserved at the Vikelaia Municipal Library of Heraklion, Crete.

Below is a chronology of the poems' composition:

1932:   [I want nothing more], [Now that calm reigns]

1933:   "Memory and Dusk," "Aerial Delicate, Light," "Anxiety"

1934:   [I'm dying, the day], [I love sleep], "Philosophy," "Myth," "Flyaways," [The sun rests on the palm of a god], [I respect the tears], [Houses that we built], [Something neutral, like slumber...]

1935:   "Designs," [Sky   crosses the ether], [The body is ready]

1936:   [I watch], [When I kissed your hair], "The Desert," [With the clarity of the seaside], [I head for the sea]

1937: "The Mist," [Should tears...], [Gardens gardens], [I feel a need to devour the days]

1938: [The bees sweetened remorse], [Dust sleep, moon], [Dawn loved], [Shadows of the other world...], "The Violets," [Rains fell upon our sea], "White Ideas"

1939: [Make way I am one], [The sea lifts her fingers...], [You let your hair loose...], [Of the efforts and the toils...], [There is a mirror within us...], [Inner diamonds], [You chop down a tree]

1940: [I sometimes wish...], [One could say...], [Come sun, my ear], [Endlessly the gulls watch...], [The sun at its zenith], [Death], [This voice is deep...], [Should we eat or should we drink...]

The prose poem quoted at the end of the introduction is "Sing" (Τραγούδα) from 1938.

George Sarantaris (1908–1941) was a Greek poet born in Constantinople and raised in Italy. After receiving a law degree from the University of Macerata, at the age of twenty-two, he moved to Greece, where he spent the rest of his life. During his time in Greece, he composed more than a thousand poems, developing a distinct poetic world that evokes the sparse, light-filled Greek landscape. He died tragically in the 1940 Greco-Italian War fighting against the country of his upbringing, Italy.

Pria Louka is a writer and translator of Greek poetry. She is the recipient of a Fulbright Fellowship that has allowed her to pursue her passion for modern Greek literature. She is the author of *The Courage to Walk and Write* (Alphabetics) and has published an extensive photographic essay on Greece. Louka, a graduate of Princeton University, currently lives in Thessaloniki, Greece.

This book is typeset in Miasma, designed by George Trian-tafyllakos for Atypical in 2020. It is an attempt to combine the idiosyncrasies of the Apla typeface style of many Greek pub-lications with the strict, upright character of Latin letterforms.

The cover is inspired by Mediterranean graphic arts of the 1930s. By that time, Modernism had been developing for de-cades across most of Europe and Art Deco was in fashion, but southern countries like Greece were latecomers and in-fused such modern styles with Italian Futurism, commercial airbrush techniques, and geometric lettering more improvi-sational than rational.

Cover design by Andrew Bourne; typesetting by Don't Look Now. Printed and bound in Lithuania by BALTO print.

 **WORLD POETRY**

Jean-Paul Auxeméry
Selected Poems
tr. Nathaniel Tarn

Maria Borio
Transparencies
tr. Danielle Pieratti

Jeannette L. Clariond
Goddesses of Water
tr. Samantha Schnee

Jacques Darras
John Scotus Eriugena at Laon
tr. Richard Sieburth

Olivia Elias
Chaos, Crossing
tr. Kareem James Abu-Zeid

Phoebe Giannisi
Homerica
tr. Brian Sneeden

Zuzanna Ginczanka
On Centaurs and Other Poems
tr. Alex Braslavsky

Nakedness Is My End:
Poems from the Greek Anthology
tr. Edmund Keeley

Jazra Khaleed
The Light That Burns Us
ed. Karen Van Dyck

Dimitra Kotoula
The Slow Horizon that Breathes
tr. Maria Nazos

Jerzy Ficowski
Everything I Don't Know
tr. Jennifer Grotz & Piotr Sommer
PEN AWARD FOR POETRY IN TRANSLATION

Antonio Gamoneda
Book of the Cold
tr. Katherine M. Hedeen &
Víctor Rodríguez Núñez

Mireille Gansel
Soul House
tr. Joan Seliger Sidney

Óscar García Sierra
Houston, I'm the Problem
tr. Carmen Yus Quintero

Maria Laina
Hers
tr. Karen Van Dyck

Maria Laina
Rose Fear
tr. Sarah McCann

Perrin Langda
A Few Microseconds on Earth
tr. Pauline Levy Valensi

Manuel Maples Arce
Stridentist Poems
tr. KM Cascia

Enio Moltedo
Night
tr. Marguerite Feitlowitz

Meret Oppenheim
The Loveliest Vowel Empties:
Collected Poems
tr. Kathleen Heil

Elisabeth Rynell
Night Talks
tr. Rika Lesser

Giovanni Pascoli
Last Dream
tr. Geoffrey Brock
RAIZISS/DE PALCHI TRANSLATION AWARD

Gabriel Pomerand
Saint Ghetto of the Loans
tr. Michael Kasper &
Bhamati Viswanathan

Rainer Maria Rilke
Where the Paths Do Not Go
tr. Burton Pike

Waly Salomão
Border Fare
tr. Maryam Monalisa Gharavi

George Sarantaris
Abyss and Song: Selected Poems
tr. Pria Louka

Seo Jung Hak
The Cheapest France in Town
tr. Megan Sungyoon

Ardengo Soffici
Simultaneities & Lyric Chemisms
tr. Olivia E. Sears

Ye Lijun
My Mountain Country
tr. Fiona Sze-Lorrain

Paul Verlaine
Before Wisdom: The Early Poems
tr. Keith Waldrop & K. A. Hays

Uljana Wolf
kochanie, today i bought bread
tr. Greg Nissan

Verónica Zondek
Cold Fire
tr. Katherine Silver